I0820112

Talking Books

Audiobook Inventor Dr. Robert B. Irwin and a New Way to Read

written by
Jenny Lacika

illustrated by
Ashanti Fortson

Atheneum Books for Young Readers
NEW YORK · AMSTERDAM/ANTWERP · LONDON
TORONTO · SYDNEY/MELBOURNE · NEW DELHI

Robert Benjamin Irwin loved to learn and explore.

When he spotted a bird swoop and settle into a crevice on the coast, he would climb up, up, up to peek into the nest.

Growing up among towering trees, in a place mainly accessible by boat, he was always looking for something new.

But when Robert was five, his eyes grew red and painful and his body burned with fever.

Soon his entire world went dark.

Robert couldn't *look* for something new now, but that didn't stop him from finding new things to discover.

He could *hear* the splash of the surf on the shore,

the squirrels skittering in circles around the trees,

the crunch of leaves beneath his feet,

and . . . the birds.

Now, rather than peeking inside nests, Robert listened and learned to discern the sounds and songs of different birds.

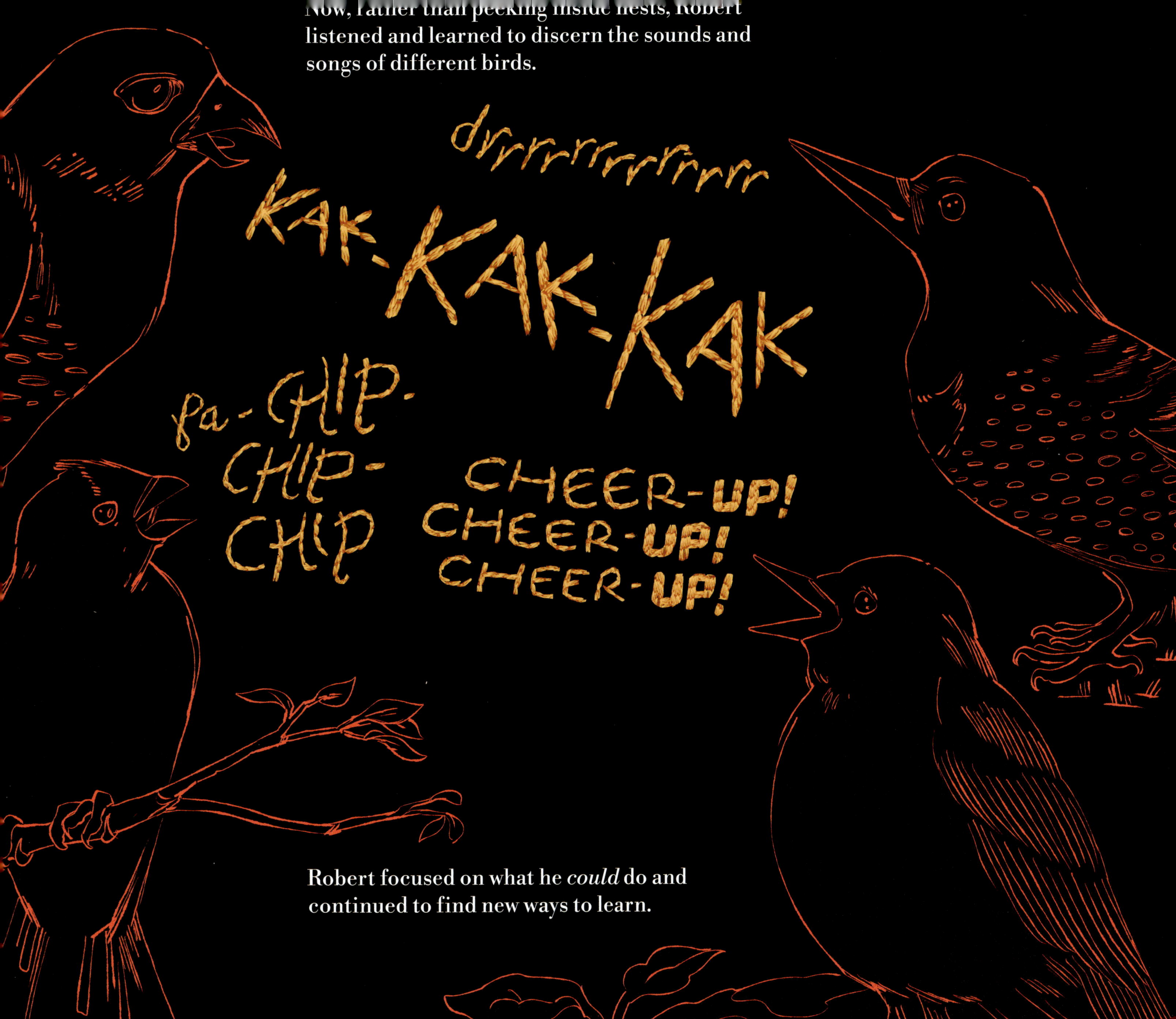

Robert focused on what he *could* do and continued to find new ways to learn.

When Robert was ready to start school, he discovered a problem. Nobody nearby had ever taught someone who learned like he did. They didn't even have books he could read.

But Robert was ready to explore something new, even if it meant a big change.

So Robert left for a boarding school
for children with disabilities.

Away from the birds.
Away from his family.

At boarding school, Robert learned to finger-read raised text, like Moontype, Boston Line Type, and braille.

He loved literature but found finger-reading difficult and slow.

Robert wished he could listen to a story like he listened to the birds. He dreamed of recordings—stories that spoke the words aloud—to play whenever he wanted. Talking books.

But recordings were short, like a song or a poem, not a full novel.

Still, Robert focused on what he *could* do to speed up his reading.

He saved pennies to pay other faster finger-readers to narrate books to him.

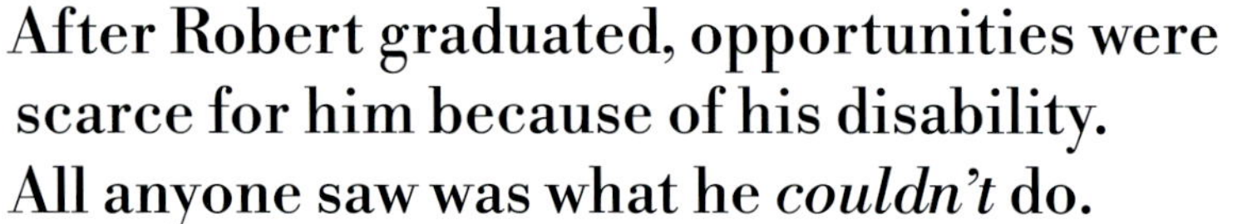

After Robert graduated, opportunities were scarce for him because of his disability. All anyone saw was what he *couldn't* do.

His family thought he could make a living playing music for spare change. But Robert wasn't done learning and exploring. He believed he could create *new* opportunities.

He worked his way up to the University of Washington, up to Harvard University, up to a job in the Cleveland public school system.

Robert proved to everyone what he could do!

Now he began to focus on what he could do for *others*.

Robert remembered how it felt to return home for the summer to the sounds of his brothers and sisters who lived there year-round.

And how it felt to leave again in the fall.

Robert didn't think children should have to choose between an education and a life at home, so he helped blind students in Cleveland attend public schools near their families, getting them the teachers, tutors, and materials they needed. Including books they could read.

Robert's success caught the attention of a new organization, the American Foundation for the Blind. They asked him to use his expertise to explore more ways to improve the lives of blind Americans.

Led by his love of literature, Robert surveyed libraries across the country. He found that very few blind readers were interested in borrowing books.

But Robert knew the problem wasn't the readers—it was the books.

These readers did not want schoolbooks or books that blind people *should* read. They wanted new books, like:

a popular author's latest mystery,

the scandalous novel making the news,

or the bestselling story about a soldier's experience during the war.

Robert came up with a plan to create a braille library full of new books for readers.

He testified in front of members of the United States Congress, and as a result, the National Library Service, a braille library for blind readers nationwide, was created.

But Robert knew there was still more he could do.

Robert soon learned that only two out of every ten blind adults in the United States could even read braille. They still had to rely on family, friends, volunteers, or paid readers to narrate books, just like Robert had when he was in school. They couldn't use the new library at all!

What they needed were the talking books Robert had dreamed about as a child.

Robert knew he could make that dream a reality.

Robert found an engineer who had invented a way to record a novel on just a handful of records. The man let Robert use his invention for free.

But when Robert approached record companies for help producing these talking books, they all said no. They said the records wouldn't make them any money.

So Robert hired a team of engineers and did it himself.

After all his hard work, it was finally time to share talking books with readers—except Congress would not add them to the National Library Service.

These new records were designed to spin at a slower speed than most, so readers didn't have machines to play them. With nothing to play on the machines, readers had no reason to buy them.

Still, that didn't stop Robert. He reached out to people across the country, convincing them to donate small amounts of money, raising enough to make six hundred machines. Enough for Congress to add talking books to the Library.

Readers who couldn't read other books *could* read these!

And they raved about the records.

Robert had discovered a new way to read. One that could even do things that print and braille books could not, like allow readers to hear the sounds and songs of birds in a birding guide.

KAK-KAK-KAK

drrrrrrrrrrrrrrrrrrr

pa-CHIP-CHIP-CHIP

CHEER-UP! CHEER-UP! CHEER-UP!

Soon other people began to discover what these books could do . . .

noon!
ss...
...Trees swaying in unison...
...it was magic!

all because Robert discovered what *he* could do.

Author's Note

I was originally drawn to the story of talking books because of my childhood love of audiobooks. I listened for hours and hours to records from yard sales and tapes my mom recorded. I was born with strabismus, and audiobooks were a way for me to read even when my eyes were tired and couldn't stay focused on the text. But the more I learned about Robert, the more I connected with him and the origins of the audiobook. Robert's disability led him to create something that he otherwise wouldn't have because his experiences gave him new perspective and knowledge. I began writing for children after I was diagnosed with multiple sclerosis and struggled with fatigue and cognitive changes that made my former career more of a challenge. Like Robert, my disability led me to something great—and now I love writing so much, I can't imagine doing anything else!

Universal Design

Although talking books were designed to benefit blind readers, they resulted in technology that benefits all readers to this day. They are an example of universal design, meaning something that is created to be accessible to the greatest number of people. Other examples of universal design—originally created for people with disabilities—are electric toothbrushes that clean teeth better with less effort; bendable straws that allow drinking from different positions; captions on videos that allow viewing in a noisy room, with the sound off, or by people learning the language; automatic doors that don't require a free hand to open; safer subway platforms; and curb cuts and ramps that make travel easier for kids on roller skates or scooters, babies in strollers, and people with limited mobility. You may be surprised by just how many things we use every day that were originally designed for people with disabilities, because universal design is good design!

Not everybody can be accommodated the same way. Curb cuts, designed for wheelchair users, were originally a hazard for blind and low-vision pedestrians who weren't able to tell when the sidewalk was ending, but the addition of tactile pavement inserts helps warn people when they are approaching the street—even if they are just busy looking at their phones! And sometimes universal design means having options, like a book available in print, audio, and braille.

More About Robert

Robert's fight for accessibility began with himself, but as he opened new doors, he wasn't content with letting them shut behind him. He wanted to open them even wider. Permanently.

Once Robert decided to improve accessibility, he devoted his life to it. One of Robert's greatest achievements was the talking book. The program more than doubled library circulation for blind readers, and the response was overwhelmingly positive. But Robert's quest for accessibility didn't just affect blind readers. The government, initially refusing to provide talking book machines to readers, changed their course and started producing the machines in the mid-1930s. Likewise, commercial publishing, having initially seen talking books as a losing proposition, has turned audiobooks into a billion-dollar-a-year industry. Some of Robert's other literary accomplishments include founding one of the first large-type publishers to produce books for low-vision students, working to improve interpointing (embossing braille on both sides of the paper) to reduce the cost and size of braille books, and helping to create a uniform type for all English-speaking countries so braille books could be shared.

Of course, Robert didn't achieve everything alone. He made a name for himself in Cleveland and then was asked to join the newly formed American Foundation for the Blind, or AFB, where he had a chance to make change on a national scale. In this story, I focused on Robert, even when he was working on behalf of the AFB, because he was recognized as the driving force behind much of the progress they made at the time.

Robert's work extended far past books, though. M. C. Migel, the first chairperson of the AFB, said, "Dr. Irwin spent himself in planning and furthering one idea after another for the benefit of his fellow blind—conservation of sight, education, gainful employment, financial assistance, legislation, etc. He exhausted his abundant energies in ceaseless and untiring labors for the blind." Robert recognized that as information and technology improved, the lives of blind people could also improve. In an interview, Robert described himself as "dark blind" (unable to see any light or shape) but said that "enough [was] known about eyes [by 1942] so that in most cases at least some sight—enough to distinguish light—[could] be saved," which may have been at least partly attributed to Robert's sight conservation efforts!

But even in his personal life, Robert was not content living according to others' expectations. While in Cleveland, Robert fell in love with a woman who worked for the Cleveland Society for the Blind. His friends discouraged him, telling him that the beautiful sighted woman had many admirers and therefore wouldn't choose Robert. But it was Robert, with his incredible ambition and drive, who caught her attention and married her. He never allowed other people to tell him what he was capable of—he was always intent on discovering for himself.

To Mom, who always made sure
I had something great to read
—J. L.

To my mom, for showing me how to never
stop learning about the world
—A. F.

ATHENEUM BOOKS FOR YOUNG READERS
An imprint of Simon & Schuster Children's Publishing Division
1230 Avenue of the Americas, New York, New York 10020

The text for this book was set in Libre Bodoni.
The illustrations for this book were rendered digitally with embroidered elements.
Manufactured in China
1025 SCP
First Edition
2 4 6 8 10 9 7 5 3 1
Library of Congress Cataloging-in-Publication Data
Names: Lacika, Jenny author | Fortson, Ashanti illustrator
Title: Talking books : Audiobook inventor Dr. Robert B. Irwin and a new way to read / Jenny Lacika ; illustrated by Ashanti Fortson.
Description: First edition. | New York : Atheneum Books for Young Readers, 2026. | Audience term: Children | Audience: Ages 4 to 8. | Summary: "This biography details how perpetually curious Robert B. Irwin found new ways to learn and explore the world after losing his sight at a young age, ultimately making stories accessible to readers of all abilities through the creation of the first audiobooks"—Provided by publisher
Identifiers: LCCN 2023026708 | ISBN 9781665912679 (hardcover) | ISBN 9781665912686 (ebook)
Subjects: LCSH: Irwin, Robert B., 1883–1951—Juvenile literature | Blind—United States—Biography—Juvenile literature | Educators—United States—Biography—Juvenile literature | Talking books—Juvenile literature | Blind—Books and reading—Juvenile literature | LCGFT: Biographies | Picture books
Classification: LCC HV1624 .I79 L33 2026 | DDC 362.4/1092—dc23/eng/20250320
LC record available at https://lccn.loc.gov/2023026708